# A Day in the Life: Sea Animals

# Dolphin

Louise Spilsbury

**www.raintreepublishers.co.uk**
Visit our website to find out
more information about
Raintree books.

**To order:**
☎ Phone 0845 6044371
📄 Fax +44 (0) 1865 312263
✉ Email myorders@raintreepublishers.co.uk

Customers from outside the UK please telephone +44 1865 312262

Raintree is an imprint of Capstone Global Library Limited,
a company incorporated in England and Wales having
its registered office at 7 Pilgrim Street, London, EC4V 6LB
– Registered company number: 6695582

Edited by Sian Smith, Nancy Dickmann, and Rebecca Rissman
Designed by Joanna Hinton-Malivoire
Picture research by Mica Brancic
Production by Victoria Fitzgerald
Originated by Capstone Global Library Ltd
Printed and bound in China by South China Printing
Company Ltd

ISBN 978 1 4062 1701 8 (hardback)
14 13 12 11 10
10 9 8 7 6 5 4 3 2 1

ISBN 978 1 4062 1885 5 (paperback)
15 14 13 12 11
10 9 8 7 6 5 4 3 2 1

**British Library Cataloguing in Publication
Data**
Spilsbury, Louise.
  Dolphin. -- (A day in the life. Sea animals)
  1. Dolphins--Pictorial works--Juvenile literature.
  I. Title II. Series
  599.5'3-dc22

**Acknowledgements**
We would like to thank the following for permission to
reproduce photographs: Ardea p.18 (© Augusto Stanzani);
Corbis p.13 (Stuart Westmorland); FLPA pp.15 (Minden
Pictures/Flip Nicklin), 17 (Terry Whittaker); Image Quest
Marine pp.7, 21, 23: flipper (James D. Watt), 10 (V&W/
Mark Conlin); Nature Picture Library p.16 (© Dan Burton);
Photolibrary pp.4 (imagebroker.net), 5 (Britain on View/
Splashdown Direct), 6 (Pacific Stock/Dave Fleetham), 8
(WaterFrame - Underwater Images/Reinhard Dirscherl), 9
(age fotostock/Fco Javier Gutierrez), 11 (Corbis), 12 (Oxford
Scientific Films (OSF)/Splashdown Direct), 14 (WaterFrame
- Underwater Images/Wolfgang Poelzer), 19 (Corbis), 23:
breathe (Britain on View/Splashdown Direct), 23: calf (Corbis),
23: dorsal fin (Oxford Scientific Films (OSF)/Splashdown
Direct), 23: pod (WaterFrame - Underwater Images/Reinhard
Dirscherl; Photoshot/NHPA) pp.20, 23: surface (Annelene
Oberholzer); Shutterstock pp.22, 23: blowhole (Kristian
Sekulic).

Cover photograph of a jumping dolphin reproduced
with permission of Corbis (© Image Source). Back cover
photograph of a blowhole reproduced with permission of
Shutterstock (© Kristian Sekulic). Back cover photograph
of teeth reproduced with permission of Corbis (© Stuart
Westmorland).

We would like to thank Michael Bright for his invaluable help
in the preparation of this book.

Every effort has been made to contact copyright holders
of material reproduced in this book. Any omissions will
be rectified in subsequent printings if notice is given to the
publisher.

All the Internet addresses (URLs) given in this book were valid
at the time of going to press. However, due to the dynamic
nature of the Internet, some addresses may have changed, or
sites may have changed or ceased to exist since publication.
While the author and publisher regret any inconvenience this
may cause readers, no responsibility for any such changes can
be accepted by either the author or the publisher.

# Contents

What is a dolphin? . . . . . . . . . . . . . . . . . . . . 4

What do dolphins look like?. . . . . . . . . . . . . 6

What do dolphins do all day? . . . . . . . . . . 8

How do dolphins swim?. . . . . . . . . . . . . . . 10

What do dolphins eat? . . . . . . . . . . . . . . . 12

How do dolphins hunt? . . . . . . . . . . . . . . . 14

When do dolphins play? . . . . . . . . . . . . . . 16

What are dolphin babies like? . . . . . . . . . 18

What do dolphins do at night?. . . . . . . . . 20

Dolphin body map . . . . . . . . . . . . . . . . . 22

Glossary. . . . . . . . . . . . . . . . . . . . . . . . . 23

Find out more . . . . . . . . . . . . . . . . . . . . . 24

Index . . . . . . . . . . . . . . . . . . . . . . . . . . . 24

Some words are shown in bold, **like this**.
You can find them in the glossary on page 23.

# What is a dolphin?

Dolphins are animals that live in oceans all over the world.

Dolphins can live close to land or swim far out in the ocean.

blowhole

Dolphins swim and feed in the ocean but they **breathe** air.

A dolphin breathes through a **blowhole** on its head.

# What do dolphins look like?

bottlenose dolphin

There are many different types of dolphin.

They may be black, white, grey, striped, or even spotty.

dorsal fin

flipper

tail

Bottlenose dolphins have curved **flippers**, a **dorsal fin**, and a tail.

They have a thick layer of fat under their skin to keep them warm.

# What do dolphins do all day?

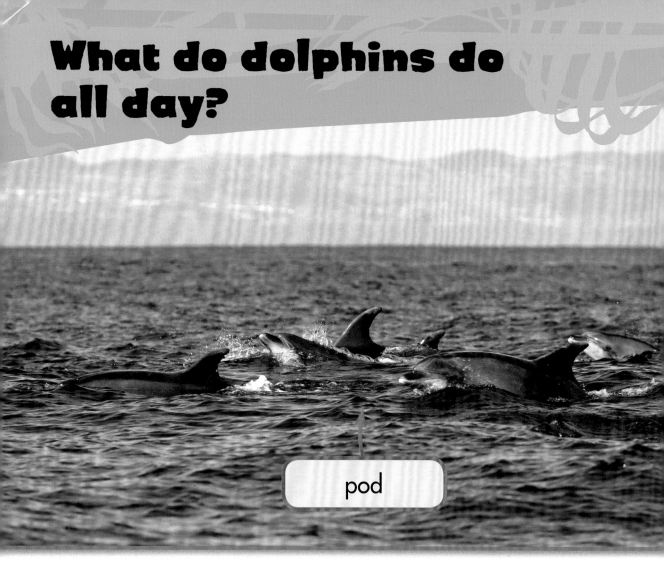

pod

Bottlenose dolphins mainly hunt for food in the morning and afternoon.

Dolphins live and hunt in groups called **pods**.

Dolphins squeak and grunt to tell each other things.

They also snap their mouths and smack the water with their tails.

# How do dolphins swim?

Dolphins move their tails up and down to swim forwards.

They use their **flippers** to turn, steer, and stop.

Dolphins dive under the water to find food.

A bottlenose dolphin can hold its breath underwater for up to ten minutes.

# What do dolphins eat?

Dolphins eat small fish, squid, and shrimps.

Dolphins use their sharp teeth to grip slippery sea animals.

teeth

Dolphins do not use their teeth to chew or cut up their food.

They swallow their food whole.

# How do dolphins hunt?

Dolphins make sounds when they hunt.

The sounds bounce back and tell the dolphins where there is food to eat.

Bottlenose dolphins swim in circles around a group of fish.

They trap the fish and take turns to swim in and catch one.

# When do dolphins play?

In the day, dolphins often play together after they have eaten.

Playing helps dolphins learn hunting skills.

Dolphins race and chase each other.

They also jump out of the water and ride on waves.

# What are dolphin babies like?

calf

A dolphin baby is called a **calf**.

A calf drinks milk from its mother's body.

A calf grows teeth to eat fish when it is about four months old.

A calf's mother and other dolphins teach it how to catch food.

# What do dolphins do at night?

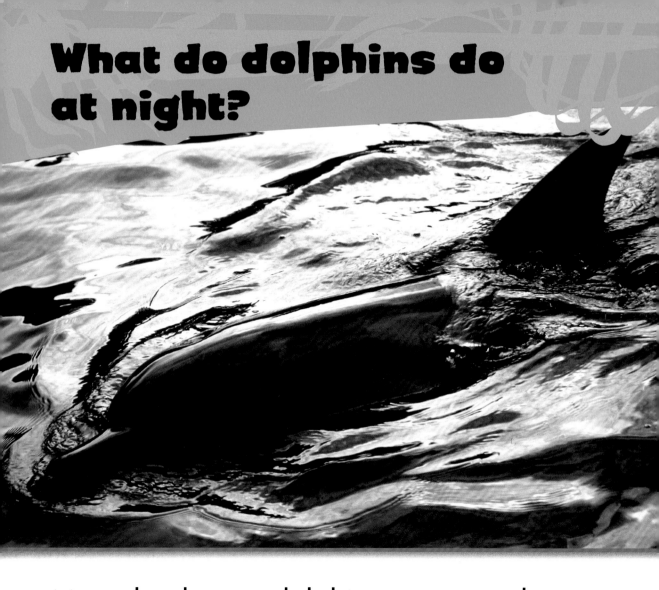

Many bottlenose dolphins rest at night.

They rest at the **surface** of the sea.

Dolphins cannot go into a deep sleep.

When dolphins rest, half their brain sleeps and the other half stays awake.

# Dolphin body map

dorsal fin

blowhole

tail

eye

flipper

# Glossary

 **blowhole** hole in the top of a dolphin's head for breathing

 **breathe** to take air into the body

 **calf** baby dolphin

 **dorsal fin** thin, flat part that sticks up from a dolphin's back

 **flipper** flat part of a dolphin's body that it uses for swimming

 **pod** group of dolphins

 **surface** top of the water

# Find out more

## Books

*Dolphin* (Natural World), Nic Davies (Wayland, 2000)
*Dolphins* (Ocean Life), Martha E. H. Rustad (Capstone Press, 2001)

## Websites

Watch a video on bottlenose dolphins and find out about them at: **kids. nationalgeographic.com/Animals/CreatureFeature/Bottlenose-dolphin**

Listen to the noises different dolphins make at: **seaworld.org/animal-info/ sound-library/index.htm**

# Index

babies  18, 19
blowhole  5, 22
breathing  5, 11
calves  18, 19
dorsal fin  7, 22
flippers  7, 10, 22
hunting  8, 11, 12, 13,
    14, 15

playing  16, 17
pod  8
resting  20, 21
swimming  4, 5, 10, 15
teeth  12, 13, 19